MONEY

DAVE ALESE

Contents

Acknowledgments

Writing this book, "Money Matters," has been fun. I've been fortunate to have the support of some incredible individuals who have made this project easy.

A big shoutout to Funmi Adeyemi for her initial editing of the manuscript.

Thank you to Sinmi Ojo for her final reviews and the adept management of the production process.

To the members of Global Harvest Maryland US, thank you for letting me be myself and for making the Pastorate work evident in your lives. You all are incredible role models.

I am also grateful to Dr. Sam Adeyemi for imparting your invaluable knowledge about money and money management. Your teachings over the years made a profound impact on me as a teenager.

Last but the best, a special thank you to Nike Alese and our kids for your consistent love, patience, and understanding that sustains me through countless hours of work and time away from home.

To every person who may not be named but have played a part in this journey, thank you from the bottom of my heart. Your contributions have made "Money Matters" a reality, and I am grateful for your kindness, support, and friendship.

Cheers to us, and to the exciting adventures that lie ahead of my publishing journey!

Introduction

Money, oh money! One topic we can all agree is as vast as the ocean and as tricky as a maze; one everyone talks about, yet only a few truly understand. That one tool that answers all yet its abuse can destroy everything.

There are so many misconceptions about the significance of money, especially among Christians. It almost feels like there's a veil of misunderstanding surrounding this glittery subject. Sadly, many of us have found it hard to understand that **MONEY MATTERS** not only to us but also to God.

Think about this! Many chapters of the Bible gave an explicit detail on the wealth of your favourite Bible characters. Beyond, Christ parables often had to do with wealth/ money management in relation to the kingdom of heaven. Confirming that a positive money management mindset is of course His expectation for us.

Throughout scripture, blessings and generosity are intertwined with the concept of wealth. In 2 Corinthians 9:6–7, we are encouraged to give cheerfully, for God loves a cheerful giver. This passage emphasises the joyful act of generosity, highlighting the reciprocal nature of blessings–one that flows both inward and outward, enriching the giver and the receiver alike.

Beyond, we are shown how wealth management is stewardship–the responsible management of God–given resources. In the Parable of the Talents (Matthew 25:14–30), Jesus illustrates the importance of faithful stewardship, commending those who multiply their talents and condemning the one who buries him out of fear. This parable emphasises accountability and diligence in utilising the resources entrusted to us, including financial assets. Instead of viewing wealth as inherently sinful, we are called to manage it wisely, recognizing our role as stewards rather than owners.

The divine partnership in the acquisition of material resources highlights God's provision and blessing to us, His people. Money, far from being a taboo topic, holds significance both to us and to God. By embracing the principles highlighted in this book, I believe that you would be able to navigate the complexities of money with intentionality, integrity and purpose.

I encourage you to read this book with an open heart and to get the most out of it. Be willing to put the principles into practice. Keep it in your library for reference and you may also give out copies to friends, proteges, colleagues, loved ones, and all those who may need it.

I cannot wait to see you thrive!

Now, let's get to where MONEY MATTERS

Money Matters

"The apostles returned to Jesus from their ministry tour and told him all they had done and taught. Then Jesus said, "Let's go off by ourselves to a quiet place and rest awhile." He said this because there were so many passers-by that Jesus and his apostles didn't even have time to eat. So, they left by boat for a quiet place where they could be alone. But many people recognized them and saw them leaving, and people from many towns ran ahead along the shore and got there ahead

of them. Jesus saw the huge crowd as he stepped from the boat, and he had compassion on them because they were like sheep without a shepherd. So, he began teaching them many things. Late in the afternoon his disciples came to him and said, "This is a remote place, and it's already getting late. Send the crowds away so they can go to the nearby farms and villages and buy something to eat." But Jesus said, "You feed them." "With what?" they asked. "We'd have to work for months to earn enough **money** *to buy food for all these people!" "How much bread do you have?" he asked. "Go and find out." They came back and reported, "We have five loaves of bread and two fish." Then Jesus told the disciples to have the people sit down in groups on the green grass. So, they sat down in groups of fifty or a hundred. Jesus took the five loaves and two fish, looked up toward heaven, and blessed them. Then, breaking the loaves into pieces, he kept giving the bread to the* *disciples so they could distribute it to the people. He also divided the fish for everyone to share. They all ate as much as they wanted, and afterward, the disciples picked up twelve baskets of leftover bread and fish. A total of 5,000 men and their families were fed."*

Mark 6:30–44 (NLT)

I don't know about you but, I just love how the scriptures identify with the realities of our everyday life. In the passage above, something important was mentioned in the conversation between the Lord Jesus Christ and his disciples. The same is observed in the book of Matthew 17: 24–27 where Jesus and Peter were accosted about paying the temple tax. The two passages had something in common.

Money.

Even though this was the Son of God who had come from heaven where the streets are made of gold, the matter of money where Jesus was concerned was never swept under the carpet, pulverised by prayer, cast out as evil, or dismissed supernaturally into nothingness. While on earth, the Lord Jesus knew money was necessary for ministry and He had followers who of their own will gave of their substance to support the ministry.

Money Matters.

Money does matter.

The scriptures say in Ecclesiastes 7:12 (KJV) that just as wisdom is a defence, *money is a defence.*

That legal tender that gets things done on behalf of the payer sure matters and matters a great deal.

Let's keep in mind the aforementioned passage in Mark 6:30–44 as we would be referring to it throughout this book. In that piece of scripture, Jesus saw the need to feed the multitude. The disciples saw this as the ultimate 'mission impossible'. This reveals to us first and foremostly that Jesus and his disciples were thinking from two different perspectives, or better still, mentalities. While the former conceived His thought from a place of over–abundance, the latter thought from a place of 'not enough'. The former focused and reached out to an endless source while the latter paid undivided attention to the limited resources available on the ground. The mindset 'litmus test' occurred when Jesus asked in paraphrased terms, "How much do you currently have?".

While the miracle of feeding the multitude is recorded as one of the several awesome works of Jesus on the earth, I'd like you to picture how this story would have been written if the mindset of lack or not–enough was allowed to prevail on that day. Regardless of the presence of the 'lack' mindset, the mindset of overabundance saved the day.

Great people, I declare to you that the journey to abundance begins with **a mindset shift.**

Building wealth, as God ordained it to be for His children, starts with having a mindset reset. It starts with dumping the mindset of lack and adopting the mindset of increase.

The first charge God gave after making man as found in Genesis 1:28 begins with–"Be fruitful and multiply; fill the earth…"

God's vision or mindset towards mankind is that of increase and this is predominantly why He wants us to have the same mindset and vision. The mindset of increase resonates with the will of God for mankind.

The mindset of increase sees opportunities instead of problems. It sees an occasion to increase solutions every time a challenge shows up.

This was the mindset Jesus had.

Your mindset affects your vision. Your vision determines your provision.

Jesus didn't depend on what was available before he decided that he needed to feed the multitude. He allowed Himself to be consumed by the vision of feeding the multitude, and by that vision, He drew resources from a place of overabundance of provision.

Provision simply means resources allocated for (pro/ in favour of) the vision.

"What do you have?"

In paraphrased terms, Jesus asked His disciples this question, as seen in the starting passage found in Mark chapter 6. Of course, He was aware that His disciples didn't have a clandestine bakery with thousands of loaves of bread stashed away; neither did He assume that they had a boat of fish waiting to be cooked and devoured. He only asked to find out the substance they had in their hearts and the state of their minds. He wanted to reveal the vision of their hearts to know if they were willing to have an iota of faith that the multitude could be fed. *Do you see these people fed and taken care of?* He wanted to know.

In other words, Jesus asked his disciples that day, "What *mindset* or *vision* do you have?"

How many times have you dreamt of something big, and almost immediately, you develop a 'mind–attack'? In this case, your mind would either attack you by declaring explicitly that you can never achieve it or attack you by asking how you would go about achieving it. The former attack comesas a negative exclamation with a full stop, while the latter poses itself as a question that sets in motion a chain of prospective ideas and thoughts.

In my opinion, the latter is a good sign. It signifies the availability of the possibility mindset which can be cultivated towards results because it naturally gravitates towards resourcefulness while the mind–attack towards impossibility repels resources without even knowing it. It may look little but this possibility mindset is that baby step on your journey towards success. Harness it!

It is critical to note that even if you think you don't have anything, your mindset, your vision, your thoughts, or your beliefs are the intangible resources that can be converted into what you can tangibly possess.

Negative beliefs will never be productive, not with God or with man. Doubt is one counterproductive belief whose effect is highlighted in James 1:5–8 (NLT):

"5 If you need wisdom, ask our generous God, and he will give it to you. He will not rebuke you for asking. 6 But when you ask him, be sure that your faith is in God alone. Do not waver, for a person with divided loyalty is as unsettled as a wave of the sea that is blown and tossed by the wind. 7 Such people should not expect to receive anything from the Lord. **8** Their loyalty is divided between God and the world, and they are unstable in everything they do".

Our prayers and our mindset/belief systems need to function in sync. If our thoughts, mindsets or beliefs are negative, they have the power to sabotage our positive desires, even the ones said in prayers. On the contrary, if our mindsets/ beliefs align and are not only positive but also rooted in God's word, they position us for *possibilities*.

The Tower of Babel of Genesis 11 is another story that amplifies the power of strong mindsets/ thoughts. God had to "come down to see the city and the tower which the children of men built" and He had to admit in the 6th verse that:

"Indeed, the people are one and they all have one language, and this is what the begin to do; NOW NOTHING THEY SET OUT TO DO WILL BE IMPOSSIBLE FOR THEM".

Your mindset and your dreams or desires must be in unison and they must speak the same language of possibility. They must be one. Don't 'miraculously' hope for one thing when in actuality, you believe the opposite.

If you truly desire a future of supernatural abundance, you cannot enter into it with a mindset of lack. Something's got to give.

May I ask a question? What do you *honestly* believe about money?

At this time, it is important to run a quick check to see the core beliefs you have about this thing called money and about the idea of finances as a whole. Your core beliefs about finances will dictate how you earn, spend, save and share your resources. Your financial status today is a reflection of your core beliefs and a showcase of just how they have shaped your wealth system over time.

Seeing that our behaviours are products of the most predominant belief systems in our lives, we must examine such beliefs to see which work against us and which empower us–and more importantly, the beliefs which align with the word of God as well as those that do not, no matter how prevalent they are in society. Join in as we identify these strongholds.

The Common Negative Beliefs about money and finances:

1. "Jesus was poor"
2. "The Word of God says we should ask God to "give us this day our daily bread" and aspire for nothing more"
3. "Wealthy people are opportunists, materialistic and ungodly."
4. "If I have abundance, my family and friends might envy me."
5. "Money will change who I am."
6. "Wealthy people are not happy."
7. "It is not my destiny to be rich/it is not in the 'cards' for me to live in abundance."
8. "Poor people have a closer relationship to God."

While some of these beliefs sound downright hilarious, these are some of the deeply rooted beliefs that run in the background of most minds like programs and codes run at the backend of software, controlling the entire foreground interface. They are *that* **powerful.**

To address the first negative belief: At the point of Jesus' death, the Scriptures wrote that the Roman soldiers cast lots for His tunic–denoting to us that it wasn't a mere robe to be discarded or torn. Even though this was a crucified and 'accursed' man, the soldiers realised that he wore a valuable piece of clothing. Jesus was not poor.

Do well to pull down those negative beliefs and strongholds.

How?

Pulling down negative beliefs about money and finances

First, you need to cultivate the habit of celebrating and rejoicing with legitimately wealthy people. You can never attract what you attack. You gravitate towards what you constantly celebrate because your mind subconsciously settles nicely into the idea as you involuntarily visualise the same for yourself. This is the whole truth because you are a direct product of your mind. This leads us to the second point.

Secondly, to become an attractor of resources,

you must be filled with positivity and possibility thoughts.

Proverbs 23:7 NKJV expressly states a principle that has been tried and trusted over the ages: "For as he (a man) thinks in his heart, so is he"

I'd like to refer to this as the Principle of Outward Reflection of Dominant Innermost Thoughts (ORDIT)

In elucidation, we can say that, "For as he [a man] thinks in his heart, so is he" (what a man dwells upon in his mind, he evolves into or becomes outwardly).

In other words, you only get to create the material equivalent of the depth and richness of your thought. You attract the content of your mind's imagination. Wow!

Think positive. Think possibility. Think wealth.

Invest in the health of your mind. Buy books by inspiring authors. Invest into rewiring your mindset and get down to work.

Thirdly, speak only of possibilities. Even when there's bad news all around, use your mouth to tell your ears some great news that is sure to lift your spirits. Even in the face of difficulty, speak about the potential possibilities. In the beginning, God spoke light in the face of deep darkness. Your words carry transformative power. Speak! It won't cost you a thing to speak what you desire to see as you continue to work it out.

Say the following after me:

"I deserve to be wealthy"

"I can create wealth"

"I am a solution provider to nations"

"All I see all around me are opportunities, not problems,"

"Jesus desires that I become a transgenerational blessing"

"I have the capacity and potential to become wealthy"

"I believe that God is able to do exceedingly, abundantly above all I can ask or think"

"God is able to make all grace abound towards me. I always have all sufficiency in all things and abundance for every good work"

God spoke in Deuteronomy 6:10 (NLT) to the children of Israel describing their transition into the Promised Land of Canaan as this: "The Lord your God *will soon* bring you into the land he swore to give you when he made a vow to your ancestors Abraham, Isaac, and Jacob…"

It was a matter of 'when' and not 'if'. God's plan to bring you into abundance is a matter of 'when' and not 'if'. This is the desire of God for all His children and it certainly is His desire for you.

This brings us to an important decision I'd greatly enjoin you to make at this point in this book–settle your sonship with God. The good news is that Jesus has done the most part in brokering the possibility of a Father–Son relationship for all of mankind by dying accursed in our place on the cross of Calvary. There, He paid for the sin and misdeeds of all of humanity in full and from then on, our place has been to accept all that He did on our behalf. After this, we are slated to live in the blessings and transformational benefits of His sacrifice, benefits which include a life of abundance as the book of 2 Corinthians 8 (NLT) confirms–"You know the generous grace of our Lord Jesus Christ. Though he was rich, yet for your sakes he became poor, so that by his poverty he could make you rich."

Even as we agree that money matters, let's untangle ourselves from damaging mindsets and beliefs as we align our minds with the mind of Jesus, living a life full of results.

Say this simple prayer:

Lord, give me the wisdom, knowledge, and understanding to make needful adjustments for a healthy mindset about money.

Lord, help me see surplus opportunities in seeming circumstances of 'so little'.

Real Money

What is Real Money?

The truth is real money is not the tangible paper or currency notes you spend.

Real Money is actually the corresponding value it attracts, thereby making real money a by–product of value creation. Resourceful and wealthy people recognize this truth deeply.

Money is just an exchange for value; a 'pro–vision' for the vision carried out by being a valuable person.

Before currency notes came into existence, the primary means of meeting needs was through an exchange termed 'trade by barter'. Farmers, for example, would exchange their crops at the local market one for another based on the value of each crop. If you had no crops to trade, you had no value to bring to the table. Hence, you had no business going to the market seeking an exchange.

Money was only printed for convenience. The real value is in what that piece of paper can attract in exchange.

To have a mindset of wealth, we need to think and identify ourselves in terms of the value that we represent rather than the physical cash that we possess. Once we can successfully take that mind trip and migrate to that zone, we begin to labour less on how much physical money we have, and we begin to harness the value that we can bring to the table.

The final result is that the currency called money flows in the direction of value. Hence, if you have no value to exchange, you are not eligible for wealth.

To understand this mindset better and simpler, I will

now flip that last sentence the other way around:

"Hence, if you have value to exchange, you are very eligible for wealth".

You *are* eligible to be a wealthy man or a wealthy woman!

But like Jesus, you need to have a vision first that will pull in the pro–vision. In the anchor passage in Mark, Jesus' vision was clear:

> *"Jesus saw the huge crowd as he stepped from the boat, and he had compassion on them because they were like sheep without a shepherd. So, he began teaching them many things. Late in the afternoon his disciples came to him and said, "This is a remote place, and it's already getting late. Send the crowds away so they can go to the nearby farms and villages and buy something to eat." But Jesus said, "You feed them." "With what?" they asked. "We'd have to work for months to earn enough money to buy food for*

*all these people!" "How much bread do you have?" he asked. "Go and find out." They came back and reported, "We have five loaves of bread and two fish." Then Jesus told the disciples to have the people sit down in groups on the green grass. So, they sat down in groups of fifty or a hundred. Jesus took the five loaves and two fish, looked up toward heaven, and blessed them. Then, breaking the loaves into pieces, he kept giving the bread to the disciples so they could distribute it to the people. He also divided the fish for everyone to share. They all ate as much as they wanted, and afterward, the disciples picked up twelve baskets of leftover bread and fish. **A total of 5,000 men and their families were fed."***

Mark 6:34–44 (NLT)

Catch a vision. Get a dream.

We need to learn to dream and dream big. Many

people think about how much money they want without realising that this should not be the primary concern. Find out what problem you need to solve first. Several of today's billionaires in globally relevant currencies started small not thinking about how much they wanted to earn but how many problems they needed to solve, how much value they needed to create, and the vision they desired to make possible. Millions of people simply paid for the problems these problem–solvers were solutions to, and the multiple effects of this converted the visionaries into billionaires.

They started out being deliberate and passionate about creating solutions for OTHERS and inadvertently created wealth for themselves and their generations. You too can hop on the 'Real Money' making train. Let's find out how.

How to get into an overabundant flow of finances

1. Recognize your Source:

To enter into overabundance, the starting point is to know your source. Just as an African adage says, "A river that forgets its source will run dry". Foremost, understand that your source is the God called the One Who Is More Than Enough. *The Elshaddai.*

You have a superfluous Source who is endless in resources and limitless in wealth and this was the same Father whom our Lord Jesus called upon in the story where He fed the multitudes. Jesus recognized His Source. Recognize yours.

2.   Have the right motive for abundance:

In the anchor passage in Mark, Jesus certainly wasn't going to get the supernatural supply to feed Himself fat with the multiplied food and the twelve baskets leftover! The vision of increase was for the multitude! Though the provision did not arrive according to the capacity of what was available (the initial 5 loaves and 2 fishes) but rather according to the capacity of the One who created and owns all the wheat and barley in all the fields in the world and all the fishes in the oceans and seas, something important triggered this overflow in provision.

It was the motive. The 'Why?'. The vision.

Every time you think about wealth just because of

you, you truncate the flow. The desire for wealth always has to be in order to be a blessing to others.

We must develop the 'tap' mindset. We are faucets. As long as we give water, we never run dry too.

3.   Acknowledge what you do have:

Jesus asked the disciples in other words, "*What do you have?*" Then He added, "*Go and find out.*"

Jesus is asking you the same question today. Have you found out what talents and skills you have? What kinds of resources are available to you? Unrefined/raw materials in nature? Relationships? You need something to multiply. It goes without saying that 0 x 100,000,000,000 = 0. You must discover what you do have and yes, you definitely have something. If you do not have physical money, you have a problem-solving attribute, hobby, or skill that people will be willing to pay to have you offer. Convert your skill into a valuable service, offer it for a fee and begin legitimate earning. After this, you can begin to diversify your streams of income.

4.   Create Structure for what you have:

Without structure, provision is squandered. Even God–given provision is at risk in the hands of a person who doesn't put a proper structure in place. Own all of the money in the whole world all you want; it would be gone in only a few days if you lack structure. How do I know this? After a couple of purchases from a few extra–luxurious brands, your account would be echoing in total emptiness in no time.

Before He fed the multitude, Jesus commanded them to sit in groups. He designed a structure for the provision that was in–coming.

Nothing multiplies outside of structure. 'Increase' cannot be measured without structure. Money will never be enough where structure is missing. Structure refers to a Budget or an estimation of expenditure.

Have a budget for everything. A financial budget puts needful financial structures in place which helps you attend to your needs according to their priorities and in the long run, helps you cultivate a lifestyle of prudence.

Divide your expenses into percentages of your income. Regulate what percentage goes into spending on Rent/Mortgage, Gas, Utilities, Food, Clothing, Tithes & Offerings, Giving, Savings, Investment, etc. This way, you can effectively measure how you're doing in the finance corner, celebrate your improvements and cheer yourself on for more efforts and returns to come.

Never spend before you budget. If you don't make a budget before the money comes, you won't be able to decipher how best to spend it. In fact, you'll be wondering where all the money went at the end of the day.

As your resources increase, your budget can expand accordingly.

Saving vs Giving

> *"The Lord your God will soon bring you into the land he swore to give you when he made a vow to your ancestors Abraham, Isaac, and Jacob. It is a land with large, prosperous cities that you did not build. The houses will be*

> *richly stocked with goods you did not produce. You will draw water from cisterns you did not dig, and you will eat from vineyards and olive trees you did not plant. When you have eaten your fill in this land, be careful not to forget the Lord, who rescued you from slavery in the land of Egypt. You must fear the Lord your God and serve him. When you take an oath, you must use only his name.*

Deuteronomy 6:10–13 (NLT)

Money is a sensitive subject. The Lord Jesus touched the subject of earning in many of His parables. Why? Because whether we want to admit it or not, we all need money.

Money is a defence and this has certainly been true in my own life. As a teenager, I witnessed a stream of financially strapped borrowers frequently requesting small cash loans from my dad, and from then on, I concluded that one should never, ever be without a significant emergency reserve put aside for rainy days.

Setting aside an emergency reserve became my personal culture as I grew older and I began to earn money myself. The mindset of having an emergency reserve has both an upside and a downside. On the upside, it has served as a long–standing financial 'governor' which helps me to live beneath my means. On the downside, in the past, it would hinder me from stepping out in faith and giving unto God's kingdom even when I sensed an urge from the Spirit to do so. It felt like the hardest thing to do especially when that sacrifice would eat into my bank statement and hit my reserve to a point that was below my comfort level. While this downside may have cost me some blessings, through godly role models, I sure have come a long way in becoming a better giver to the Lord, following the leading of God's Spirit as I 'walk by faith and not by sight'.

As we dig deep to build a strong financial foundation established on God's infinite supply, let's pray:

Lord, help me to trust You as my Source.

Lord, open my eyes to the right relationships and to the right information that will help to renew my mind about finances.

Lord, help me to see circumstances as You see them.

LAWS OF FINANCIAL ABUNDANCE

For the purpose of emphasis and to maintain context, let's revisit one of scriptures aforementioned:

> *"The apostles returned to Jesus from their ministry tour and told him all they had done and taught. Then Jesus said, "Let's go off by ourselves to a quiet place and rest passersby, that Jesus and his apostles didn't even have time to eat. So, they left by boat for a quiet place, where they could be alone.*

But many people recognized them and saw them leaving, and people from many towns ran ahead along the shore and got there ahead of them. Jesus saw the huge crowd as he stepped from the boat, and he had compassion on them because they were like sheep without a shepherd. So, he began teaching them many things. Late in the afternoon his disciples came to him and said, "This is a remote place, and it's already getting late. Send the crowds away so they can go to the nearby farms and villages and buy something to eat." But Jesus said, "You feed them." "With what?" they asked. "We'd have to work for months to earn enough money to buy food for all these people!" "How much bread do you have?" he asked. "Go and find out." They came back and reported, "We have five loaves of bread and two fish." Then Jesus told the disciples to have the people sit down in groups on the green grass. So, they sat down in groups of fifty or a hundred. Jesus took the five loaves and two fish, looked up toward heaven, and blessed them. Then, breaking the loaves into pieces, he kept giving the bread to the disciples so they could distribute it to the people. He also divided the fish for everyone to share. They all ate as much as they wanted, and afterward, the disciples picked up twelve baskets of leftover bread and fish. A total of 5,000 men and their families were fed."

Mark 6:30–44 (NLT)

Having experienced mind shifts in the previous pages of this book, I believe you are seeing, believing, and understanding this passage of scripture in greater light and greater faith.

In the scriptural reference, Jesus wanted to feed a multitude numbering well over 5000 people. We have since discovered that the disciples saw it as an impossible mission because they were thinking from a place of 'not enough'. Jesus had an understanding that God the Father was His Source and He knew that feeding the multitude was no big deal to His

Father. This understanding was His most innermost thought which fuelled His outward actions and was backed up by a divine manifestation of provision. Enshrined in that scriptural reference in the book of Mark are certain principles and laws that govern abundance.

We will get to them in a bit.

Laws of Abundance–Turning a little into a lot

Life is governed by laws and principles. Every time you break any of life's laws, you sabotage yourself.

Laws / Principles are powerful. They are neither respecters of persons nor do they have favourites. They stand true in every location under the sun and are unchanging in all situations.

God put universally operative principles in place all over the world so that He can have rest, else He would have had to work repetitively to keep the earth running perfectly as it is today.

An example of these principles is that of Day and Night as well as the principle of Seasons. They operate unfailingly at their appointed time of the year. Another Law, likewise, is the Law of Gravity. If you use it to your advantage, you will get the best of it. Otherwise, you could suffer for it greatly.

When it comes to principles, Ignorance is never an excuse.

Some may not agree with certain laws and some laws may make some people uneasy, but in the end, respecting governing laws, and principles of life will do you nothing but a whole world of good.

Abundance, especially Financial Abundance, is set into motion by Laws that are no respecters of persons like other Laws of life. I dare to say that even the 'rich' by today's standards continually multiply their wealth by these self–same laws that govern financial abundance else, they would be in penury quicker than you can say, "Jack". For a better understanding of the Laws of Financial Abundance, we mustexpose certain financial ideologies which may be commonplace in today's age but are not based on God's Word and God's thoughts towards us "of good and not of evil". To this end, let's practically get a hang of the Laws of Financial Abundance.

Are you ready for the truth? Let's dig in.

The 3 Laws of Financial Abundance

1. Do not borrow for consumption

What is Borrowing? Claiming things that you don't own. Owning things on credit. Possessing things in advance. Spending the money that you are yet to have to buy things you shouldn't yet consider. Borrowing sure comes in many shades and disguises but however way it presents itself, it is not a path to Abundance. It is actually headed in the opposite direction. **Do not borrow!** Jesus never considered borrowing in any situation, not even to feed the multitude. In the same scenario, the Lord's disciples also mentioned buying and not borrowing because they have been taught by Jesus not to instinctively think of borrowing as an option. American society is especially notorious for encouraging people to live a 'borrowed' lifestyle by making borrowing incredibly easy for people. People borrow the money they don't have to buy the things they don't need in order to impress the people that do not like them and that is such an anomaly.

Why do people borrow?

a.   They don't trust the process of waiting.

b.   They lack faith in God's ability to provide.

c.   They feel the need to impress other people.

d.   They have poor planning and poor budgeting skills.

e.   They do not believe in delayed gratification

The lifestyle of borrowing can be cured by:

a.   Putting in the work and trusting the process

b.   Being grateful to God for what you have.

c.   Separating wants from needs then striking out 'impressing people' from your list of needs.

d.   Making a budget for everything with the mindset that says "whatever I cannot afford right now, I do not need it right now". Think of everything you earn and spend as your income and expenditure. Make sure you end every month with a positive bottom line or else you are tailing towards a lifetime of being broke and in debt. Budget an amount for savings because by being BIG on savings, you're literally paying yourself.

> Never spend before you budget. And, no, budgeting isn't a sign of lack or having not enough. Large corporations thrive based on budgets. Developed nations of the world have a yearly budget. Budgeting isn't for poor people. Rather, it helps you become a person of great wealth. You need to budget.

Therefore, the First Law of Abundance tells us to **Renounce the Lifestyle of Borrowing.**

The singular exception to this is that borrowing is only valid when you need to acquire assets and investments or kickstart businesses in which returns are guaranteed over time. Borrowing to acquire liabilities of any kind amounts to nothing but great losses.

Assets are acquisitions that add value/money to their owners while liabilities only take money/value away from their possessors.

2.   Do not be a grumbler

Another factor contrary to the Law of Financial Abundance is Grumbling.

Grumbling means to mutter in discontent.

1 Corinthians 10:10 (NLT) says, " And don't grumble as some of them did, and then were destroyed by the angel of death."

There's nothing that kills the fastest both on earth and in the spirit realm other than grumbling or murmuring. God hates grumbling/murmuring and this is because grumbling is anti–faith. Murmuring irks God due to the fact that it directly accuses God of being a liar who is not faithful to keep His word and is not as able as He claims to be after all.

Sadly, a lot of people grumble. They complain about everything. when it's hot, they grumble: when it's cold, they murmur. Some even see complaining as a duty to fulfil and wear it as a badge of honour. Grumbling or murmuring destroys everything, even the things built legitimately by hard work.

In this kingdom–God's kingdom, it is a sin to grumble. **Thou shall not grumble.**

Life will not always look fair and grumbling sometimes feels like a natural response to our trials.

However, we handle the situation better by giving thanks in faith because we know that ultimately, God is for us.

In the central passage where He fed the multitudes, Jesus, rather than grumbling about what was not enough, gave thanks. If a lot of today's believers were in those shoes, they would have thrown a grumbling party and invited wailers to join in the spree. This wouldn't have solved anything, would it?

The central passage in Mark 6:30–44 reveals a crucial secret; thanksgiving multiples whatever is in our hands. Jesus gave thanks and heaven multiplied the resources.

The Second Law of Abundance tells us to **Maintain a Heart of Thanksgiving**

The antidote to the habit of grumbling is developing a heart of sincere thanksgiving.

Become a thanksgiving addict.

Thank God for the seemingly little things–eyes that see, ears that hear, sense of smell, the gift of taste, ability to walk around, ability to get dressed, ability to use the bathroom, ability to think straight and reason logically. The things to be thankful for far outweigh the things to complain about. One major thing about moments of heartfelt thanksgiving is that they draw the attention of heaven, the attention that years of grumbling can never garner. It may look like grumbling is the key to your desperate need for a miracle but in actual fact, Thanksgiving is the correct passcode to your miracle.

3.   Do not waste resources:

Wastage, in every form, is a destructive habit. A waster is a killer.

Wastage can be in the form of being lazy with talents or skills, being a procrastinator, being a time–waster, being an impulsive buyer, taking things for granted, treating opportunities shabbily, etc.

By all means, thou shall not waste.

We must prepare for our tomorrow today by building productive personal habits even in the days of little beginnings. One of those habits is having the custom of being a good and faithful steward/manager of available resources whether they are tangible or intangible, few or lavish.

Hence, to **be a Good Manager of available Resources** is the hallmark of the Third Law of Financial Abundance

> *"He that is faithful in that which is least is faithful also in much: and he that is unjust in the least is unjust also in much. If therefore ye have not been faithful in the unrighteous mammon, who will commit to your trust the true riches? And if ye have not been faithful in that which is another man's, who shall give you that which is your own?"*

Luke 16:10–12 NLT

God tests us with little things before He blesses us with big things.

Your current opportunities are pointers to your coming season. Not discerning them or taking them for granted will cut short your desired progress. You must take every stage you're in today as a test for the next stage. Whatever your hands find to do right now, do it with the right motive and do it with all your heart.

Train yourself to be a giver.

Put a smile on the face of another.

Give some warm food to those who have no idea where their next meal will come from.

Pay tuition for people who can't afford it.

Do what you can with what you have in the name of the Lord Jesus.

Proverbs 19:17 NLT states a principle God is bound by–" If you help the poor, you are lending to the LORD–and he will repay you!" Even unbelieving prosperous people have been beneficiaries of this principle.

From time immemorial, it's been proven that the gospel reaches more souls, and more so effectively when people are cared for. Jesus showed a perfect example of this in His ministry on earth. Of a truth, the popular quote by Theodore Roosevelt "No one cares how much you know until they know how much you care" mirrored Jesus and His ministry on earth.

Let people be able to say of you that whatever you do is done well and wholeheartedly. Whether or not you get acknowledged with a 'thumbs up' or a 'well–done', go all out to be faithful in your deeds.

Want to find out if you are faithful in your deeds? *Ask your spouse. Ask your pastor. Ask your boss.*

Take stock

Stocktaking is key in avoiding wastage. In our central passage where the multitudes were fed, it was in picking up the leftovers in avoidance of waste that the magnitude of the miracle was truly understood and further appreciated. They picked everything such that nothing was wasted and 12 baskets full of leftovers were recovered after everyone had their fill.

The disciples took stock. You need to take stock.

If you don't take stock of how your money was spent and how you arrived at your current baseline amount, you just might end up being a waster without even knowing it.

We sure have a couple of things to pray about in the light of the Laws of Financial Abundance. Let's pray:

Lord let all I have read begin to bear fruits in my heart. I refuse to be obstinate about changing any wrong habits.

Lord, show me practical ways to embrace change as regards my personal finances.

Lord give me the grace to obey the leading of your Spirit as a result of this word.

The Covenant of Wealth

"The LORD brought his people out of Egypt, loaded with silver and gold; and not one among the tribes of Israel even stumbled. Egypt was glad when they were gone, for they feared them greatly. The LORD spread a cloud above them as a covering and gave them a great fire to light the darkness. They asked for meat, and he sent them quail; he satisfied their hunger with manna—bread from heaven. He split open a rock, and water gushed out to form a river

> *through the dry wasteland. For he remembered his sacred promise to his servant Abraham.*
>
> *So he brought his people out of Egypt with joy, his chosen ones with rejoicing.*
>
> *He gave his people the lands of pagan nations, and they harvested crops that others had planted. All this happened so they would follow his decrees and obey his instructions. Praise the LORD!"*

Psalms 105:37–45(NLT)

In so many ways, the children of Israel under the Old Testament law typify us as born–again Christians living in the New Testament age of grace. While we largely differ, we also share a lot in common.

- God loved and chose them without their opinion or contribution. We are saved by grace and not our works.

- God called their father and ancestor Abraham while he was a pagan. While we were yet sinners and ungodly, Jesus died for us.

- The Israelites were in bondage in Egypt under the slave master Pharaoh just as we were also in darkness as unbelievers, being cheated and dominated by Satan.

- In the days of Israel's oppression in the land of Egypt, sickness and diseases had a field day, and lack was commonplace because until God sent Moses, Pharaoh ruled over them and oppressed them as freely as he wished. When Jesus saved us by grace, He not only saved us to have an eternal home in heaven but paid with His death and blood to give us a heaven on earth kind of life by destroying the power of sin over our lives that causes sickness, diseases and certainly poverty. The Bible says in 2 Corinthians 8:9 that, "For you know the grace of our Lord Jesus Christ, that though He was rich, yet for your sakes He became poor, that you through His poverty might become rich." Jesus left behind His most glorious existence to bring you out of a life of lack into a life of abundance.

God decided to bring His people out of Egypt and show them His intention for making them His people by bringing them into Canaan–the promised land. God wanted to lavish His love on them. Every time the Lord delivers, the plan is to bring us into something better, and for that reason, He delivered Israel from Egypt with Silver and Gold as is written in Psalm 105:37. If you could believe that God saved you from the nature of sin to bring you into His nature of righteousness, you must not find it hard to believe that you were also saved from a life of penury and brought into a life of prosperity.

Poverty is NOT the will of God

Psalm 105:35 declares that "He (God) brought them (Israel) forth also with silver and gold…". Ever wondered why God made sure to bring Israel out of slavery as a prosperous nation? Why He didn't allow them to come out of Egypt, though free but broke, busted and disgusted?

This is because poverty is still slavery. Poverty is not a gentleman; poverty is an armed man and an eventual killer.

It is such a kill joy; it kills dreams and visions. It makes people lie, it makes people die before their time, it attracts disease and gets people deceased without fulfilling their purposes. Poverty causes greed and chaos even amongst blood–related family members. Poverty, amongst several things, makes even the most romantic of relationships turn unnecessarily sour. Some people say that money cannot buy happiness. If money cannot buy happiness, the question I usually would ask is, what can lack or poverty buy? What can it afford? Absolutely nothing! Money can certainly buy certain things that make for happiness! Poverty puts mankind in a vicious cycle of frustration and hate and even makes killers out of people. Poverty is NOT the will of God.

The Plan of God is for His people to be well taken care of. To become rich enough to be comfortable. Not everyone will be a Jeff Bezos or an Elon Musk, but everyone can be self–sustainable and comfortable.

God was deliberate about the birth of Israel as a nation out of Egypt. He brought them forth with abundance and made sure they had enough. They inherited the labour of the people of Egypt. That was His deliberate plan.

Israel evolved from abject poverty as slaves in Egypt to becoming a nation abundant in Silver and Gold and finally, they settled into a land flowing with abundance; Milk and Honey.

This was the progression of Israel, the people of God:

Poverty and Slavery —> Freedom, Silver & Gold —> Land flowing with Milk & Honey.

While it was a journey, they were progressing. They progressed because one thing singled them out amongst the several nations on the earth at that time–The Covenant.

Wealth, supernatural wealth and prosperity are all covenant issues.

Why did God bless Israel? Because they were in covenant with Him.

To understand Wealth, we must understand the Covenant because this is what produces the Wealth.

> ***"But thou shalt remember the Lord thy God: for it is he that giveth* thee***

power to get wealth, that he may establish his covenant *which he sware unto thy fathers, as it is this day.*"

Deuteronomy 8:18 (KJV)

The wealth that comes from God is tied to the Covenant. If being wealthy was ungodly, then God would not give the power to get wealth.

When we understand the underlying principle of getting wealth, we agree with God on the subject of wealth being our portion. The wealth isn't just having stupendous riches, but it is peaceful abundance with nothing missing, nothing broken.

What is the Covenant about?

God wanted Abraham to become responsible and committed to the relationship they shared so He decided to establish a covenant between them.

When a man and a woman decide to get married, they cut a covenant with their vows before God and man and this covenant makes both parties become not two but one. They become responsible for and to each other regardless of any situation. A greater covenant they share is cut during marital intercourse and this is a blood covenant. This is the reason why casual premarital sex or adultery is more gravely than most people think. On the Forbes list, I noticed that certain billionaires become billionaires by the virtue of their family inheritance as it is for the Walt Disney family or Walmart family. Some others became billionaires by the virtue of marriage. Think about it! It is almost impossible to have a billionaire's wife living in penury, she automatically partakes in the wealth by marriage. This clearly explains the principle of the Covenant.

A blood covenant, in days of old, was the recognized way for two families to come into an unbreakable union. When the blood of two individuals or families intermingles in a Blood covenant, it means they become a part of each other. In this case, what belongs to one belongs to the other.

The terms and conditions sound like this: "Your battle becomes my battle, your pain becomes my pain, your family becomes my family and I will defend all that is yours as though it is mine because it now is".

God made this covenant, a blood covenant, with Abraham in Genesis chapter 17.

A blood covenant is irrevocable. This was the kind of covenant God shared with Abraham. As a result of it, Abraham became one with God.

Abraham fought 7 kings and their countless armies with 318 men. This was possible as a result of the fact that when Abraham showed up at the battle, God's army and the host of heaven were compelled to get involved because God was in a covenant with Abraham.

Think about it critically, 319 men versus 7 kings and their numerous legions of warriors. Don't ever think Abraham went into battle foolishly. He absolutely did not. Abraham had a covenant consciousness. He could see the hidden militia of his Covenant God even though others couldn't see them.

Remember the story of Elisha and his servant in the book of 2 Kings 6? Yet another story of a man who had a Covenant Partner and knew it like he knew his name.

All through the story of Abraham the friend of God, there was not a single account of Abraham being sick. There was not an account of Abraham suffering loss. Abraham became richer and richer in Silver and Gold, in cattle and sheep, in male and female servants. When Abraham's wife was taken by King Abimelech in Gen. 20, God showed up for him in Abimelech's dream. Abraham was fruitful even in old age, bearing a child when he was grey and old. Abraham died at a good old age of 175.

Abraham left a legacy of walking with God, of faith, and of prosperity by the Covenant which he passed down to generations after him.

In reiteration, therefore, Wealth is a covenant issue.

The Covenant Mindset explained

The more of the Covenant we understand and practise, the better we become. By this, you will realise that even though labour and hard work are important, they did not get you the wealth you got but because it was most importantly, as a result of the

Covenant. This is one reason why giving to God is not an issue to people who are in covenant with Him and understand the basis of the Covenant. Giving to the furtherance of God's kingdom whether as offerings, tithes, or honouring God's anointed over us comes with no stress when we are people who understand the Covenant. We know Christ gave it all up for us so giving our substance back to Him is a no–brainer because we are One with Him. All that we are and all that we have is all His as we share a covenant. Even more amazingly, all that He has is ours as a result of the same covenant.

As people in covenant with God, not just our finances but all that we represent and that represents us whether our children, our brainchildren, our businesses, our assets, our influence, our social status, our time and life are owned by God who is our Senior Partner through life. We have our share in Him as He pours out on us a lavish show of love in multiple dimensions than we can ever ask or think–in mercy, in protection, in supernatural health, in favour, in forgiveness, in power to get wealth and several countless other ways. Certain proclamations and declarations can only come from the heart and lips of a covenant–minded person. The covenant mindset makes us invoke things the way God would invoke them, to command things like God would command them, to call things forth the way He would call them forth because, by covenant, we have the mind of Christ.

Walk in the consciousness of the Covenant!

The Blessing–the Anointing for Wealth

There is an anointing for Wealth. It is a spiritual force and empowerment that comes upon covenant–minded people. Scriptures refer to this as the power to get wealth so that He may establish His covenant. Let's read that verse again but with gained insight.

> *"But thou shalt remember the Lord thy God: for it is he that giveth* **thee power to get wealth, that he may establish his covenant** *which he sware unto thy fathers, as it is this day."*

Deuteronomy 8:18 KJV

This spiritual force or power to get wealth is called

the Blessing of the Lord.

Proverbs 10:22 (NLT) reads–"The blessing of the Lord makes one rich, And He adds no sorrow with it".

The Blessing empowers the blessed with the wisdom for getting wealth, sustaining wealth, and disbursing wealth. This adds fulfilment and joy to their wealth– the fact that they can be disbursers of the abundance. This is why many people who make riches outside legitimate means and outside of the Blessing of the Lord neither succeed at keeping, multiplying, or distributing it, nor do they find any fulfilment by it.

Let's talk to our covenant—keeping God as we release our faith in the Covenant that we share with Him:

God, open my eyes to the intricate details of the Covenant wrought for me by the death of Jesus.

Help me walk in the full consciousness and understanding of Your covenant.

How to Get out of Debt

"A certain woman of the wives of the sons of the prophets cried out to Elisha, saying, "Your servant my husband is dead, and you know that your servant feared the Lord. And the creditor is coming to take my two sons to be his slaves." So, Elisha said to her, "What shall I do for you? Tell me, what do you have in the house?" And she said, "Your maidservant has nothing in the house but a jar of oil." Then he said, "Go, borrow vessels from everywhere, from all your neighbours—empty

> *vessels; do not gather just a few. 4 And when you have come in, you shall shut the door behind you and your sons; then pour it into all those vessels, and set aside the full ones." So, she went from him and shut the door behind her and her sons, who brought the vessels to her; and she poured it out. 6 Now it came to pass, when the vessels were full, that she said to her son, "Bring me another vessel." And he said to her, "There is not another vessel." So, the oil ceased. 7 Then she came and told the man of God. And he said, "Go, sell the oil and pay your debt; and you and your sons live on the rest."*

2 Kings 4:1–7 (NKJV)

In the passage above, the widow of the prophet was left not just in penury but in debt such that her sons were at risk of slavery.

Debt is an outrightly dreadful thing. Interestingly, we live in an age that is unconsciously driven towards amassing more and more debt because the more people are indebted, the more certain people, organisations, or systems flourish and thrive. Debt is perhaps one of the most discouraging things on earth and perhaps, a lot of Christians struggle with recurrent debt.

I would always say that the journey from 'here' to 'there'–the journey from where we are right now to where we desire to be–is a knowledge gap. The more of the knowledge gap we can bridge, the more successful we are. Thankfully, God the holder of all knowledge makes provisions to get people, especially His children, out of debt and we will be exploring these provisions as we gain divine perspective towards becoming debt–free.

What is Debt?

What *really* is debt?

Debt is a form of self–inflicted bondage. Debt is the procrastinator's way of spending money. When debt is hanging over a man's head, he cannot be at peace. It greatly compromises one's income stream of income and aspirations to build wealth. The previous passage in 2 King 4 wherein was the prophet's widow shows us that debt puts not only us but our loved ones in slavery. This is because every time we borrow, we put the future in deficit to spend at the moment. The late prophet in that scripture may have thought he was borrowing at his personal risk or he may have thought he was borrowing to care for his family when in actual fact, he travelled into the future to borrow thereby mortgaging the lives and freedom of his two sons to the increased sorrow of his widowed wife.

What I consider as being worse of all is this; the late prophet left behind a legacy of lack for his generations to come. Whether we like to believe it or not, without the help of additional influences in our lives, we tend towards the paths towed by our parents. The sons of the prophet, if not for the supernatural intervention of God, would have begun to think that lack, borrowing and debt were patterns of life to follow because that was how their daddy lived and eventually died. Thank God for using Elisha to lay a new foundation for these two young men about life and about finances by opening unto them a stream of earning without having to beg or owe. If not for divine intervention, I'm not sure that the late prophet would have truly rested in peace due to the untold hardship the family he left behind would be faced with.

Debt prevents rest. Debt is a sin in the Bible. The majority of the time God talks about sin, He speaks of it as a debt.

Debt does not only just compromise our ability to provide but our ability to be generous unto others. Debt is also always in strong conflict with a hard working mindset. The only tenable form of 'debt' is debt incurred when one borrows money to acquire investments or assets and not to obtain consumables.

It is not God's plan that we are suppressed with debt because it is a vicious cycle of lack which is very much unlike The Blessing which He blesses us with. If we find ourselves owing one way or another at the moment, the good news is that there's an exit door to the world of debt.

While there's no singular path, there are a few practical ways to get out of debt.

Practical ways to get out of Debt:

1. Pay off more than the minimum on your credit card: This reduces the principal amount faster which in turn reduces the interest accruing in your debt. If you don't pay more than the minimum, it could take forever to clear the debt on your credit card.

2. Spend less than you earn: The reason why you are in debt in the first place is that you spend more than you earn. The moment you make a habit out of spending more than you earn or all that you earn, it will be difficult to break that habit. Proverbs 21:20 NLT says that "The wise have wealth and luxury, but fools spend whatever they get." If the Bible declares that a foolish man spends all, how do you think it would refer to a man who not only spends all but also borrows? Even if it's as low as the equivalent of 20 dollars, do all you can to keep something reserved off every monthly salary or pay check. The aim shouldn't be just to pay off your debt but to have at least 3 to 6 months of your daily needs (shelter, food, clothing, logistics,

insurances, phone bills) in a reserve especially if you have a 9 to 5 job. Call it an 'Emergency Fund'. A wise man once said that advising 9 to 5 job employees to start a business isn't so much so that they can quit the 9 to 5 but to ensure that there is some kind of insurance to fall back on when the 9 to 5 quits on them because nothing is guaranteed in these times. After you have cleared your debt and created an Emergency fund, then invest the rest of your income. God gives bread to the eater and seed to the sower but you must identify what your bread (recurrent basic need) is and what your seed (investment) is. Come up with a budget and determine how much you need to spend per month and delineate what goes into savings.

3.   Pay up your most expensive debt first: Find out your APR on your credit card. Consolidate all your debts into one. Pay in advance and crash down the principal such that your interest accruing per day weakens and the time left to clear your debt shortens. This works for mortgages and car loans.

4. Buy a quality used pre–owned car: If you have a taste for a new car, save more aggressively to be able to afford it rather than borrow to get it.

5. Reduce the money spent on groceries by buying in bulk: This cuts down the total amount spent on monthly supplies.

6. Get a second job: Do this with a goal in mind–to clear your debt and not to get into more debt by using the extra income for acquiring unnecessities.

7. Track your spending: This way, you know what changed in your regular spending

8. Pray: God's supernatural power enables us to break free from debt. In the scriptural reference in 2 Kings 4, a supernatural provision eased the breakage of the bondage of debt in the life of the prophet's widow and her sons. Supernatural intervention has a few principles though such as Tithing. A child of God cannot be cursed but evading honouring God with tithes and giving can

make one's life look like it's cursed. In our pursuit to get out of owing, when we put God first, He provides us with supernatural provision that eases us into living free from debt.

You may have debts you need to pay up in your life and sometimes, it feels like the debts are never-ending as they keep on piling up. Let's ask for divine empowerment to live not just debt-free, but to live in plenty.

Let's pray:

*I take authority over every power of hell
causing compulsive buying and debt addiction
in my life in Jesus' name and I declare that
I am he who the Son of God has set free,
therefore I am free indeed from every such
spirit!*

*I receive divine wisdom and ease to surmount
every debt I am faced with.*

*I decree that the windows and doors of
heaven are open over my life and I receive
supernatural ideas for wealth creation and
multiplication.*

CONCLUSION

IN THESE FINAL PAGES OF "Money Matters," let's take a moment to truly grasp the essence of what we've explored together. Money, as we've come to understand, is more than just the tangible notes and coins we exchange; it's a divine tool entrusted to us by God–a symbol of dominion, and an instrument capable of shaping destinies.

Throughout our read, we have learned that our mindset on the money we own at the moment holds immense significance. How we perceive our financial resources determines whether we see challenges or opportunities, obstacles or stepping stones. This mindset affects how quick we are able to navigate our financial journey towards our goal. So constantly ask yourself what you see!

Central to our financial growth is the power of our thoughts. Our mindset and habits play pivotal roles in nurturing and sustaining the unending wealth that God has ordained for us. Regardless of how little we may seem to have now, cultivating a healthy mindset is crucial for unlocking the abundance that awaits us.

However, we cannot afford to forget that we are called to a bigger purpose. Our vision for wealth extends beyond personal gain; it is divine. Aligning our dreams with God's plan, and seeking His guidance in all aspects of our financial endeavour pave the way for His divine intervention in our lives.

In all, let us not overlook the importance of integrity and stewardship in wealth creation. Building solid principles rooted in God's Word, investing in relationships, and establishing efficient systems are essential for enduring success. Avoiding falling into the trap of indebtedness, as it only steals from our future, hindering the financial freedom that awaits us.

Take this with you: The covenant of wealth is not

exclusive; it is available to all who align themselves with God's will. By embracing this covenant, we not only secure our own prosperity but also become vessels of blessings to the world around us, leaving behind a legacy of love through the powerful tool called MONEY.

Allow me to reiterate this even for the last time in this book, MONEY MATTERS!